7 Day Ebusiness:

How You Can Build a Business Step by Step in 7 days or Less and Make Money on the Internet

by Jinger Jarrett

To get my articles, best free resources, and tips and ideas on internet marketing, small business, and writing, you can subscribe to my new blog: Internet Marketing for Free, http://www.askjinger.com.

My blog will provide you with up to the minute information on the best free tools, software, and information available and all in a nice digest format. It's a great five minute read that will save you hours in reading time.

Published by Create Space
ISBN: 1440415080
EAN-13: 9781440415081

About Me

My name is Jinger Jarrett. I have been in business for myself for several years now.

When I first started off on the Internet, I hardly knew how to use a browser or email. Originally I came on the Internet to use it to promote a business venture I was working offline. That business venture fell apart, the company also failed, and I was out a lot of money.

My education background is Journalism and English. I'm a writer, not an internet marketer. I prefer spending my time writing than marketing, and that can be a problem because if you don't market; it's very hard to make any money from your business.

After the business venture I was in failed, I started doing my homework. I bought a lot of ebooks and software, but I never really did anything with them. During 2003, I started using articles to promote my business. I created newsletters actually using autoresponders. I taught myself how to write HTML, and I started building websites.

In the beginning my sites were pretty ugly. They looked very amateurish. I didn't understand the fundamental techniques of creating a business website.

I kept learning, and I kept trying. Using articles, I promoted my websites and kept refining them. I started to make money, and I've been making money ever since.

Now, website owners from all over the world ask for my articles. I've been read in over 40 countries by over one million people.

Currently, I am the lead expert panel member for **NetProfitSecrets.com.**

The point is, you can succeed on the Internet. It isn't easy. You have to work hard. It isn't easy to start a business, online or offline. There is, however, a simple formula, you can follow, step by step to get your business set up quickly. Stay focused, ignore a lot of the phony trends you see online, and you will succeed.

I wrote this ebook to save you years of frustration. This book isn't just about making money. It's about me helping others because I understand the frustration involved in starting a business. I also want to provide my readers and clients with top notch products and services that will really help you in your business building ventures.

Table of Contents

Getting Started

Please note: Every resource that is included in this book is something that I have used. I also own all of the software that I recommend. I don't see the point of trying to sell something that you really don't know anything about. All of my recommendations are based on results I have received from using each resource. You do not have to buy or own these resources to be successful online. I have only provided these resources in case you need more help. Also, many of the resources available in this ebook are free, so please feel free to pick and choose based on where you are at in your business.

Let me emphasize this: you have to decide which is more important: time or money. Starting off, you will be investing more time than money. Once you have invested your time and made the money, then you can invest your money in time saving tools. You are building a business here, and the whole process occurs in steps. It took a long time before I could afford to acquire these tools. As I have acquired new tools, it has saved me time and money, and I have been able to focus more on marketing.

The only exception I make here is buying a domain and web hosting. These are absolutely crucial to your success because it gives you competitive advantage over everyone else, especially if you market affiliate programs. Investing in a domain and paid web hosting shows potential customers you are serious about your business.

With all of the changes in Google Ad Words, as well as most sites requiring a landing page instead of being able to refer your customer directly to the merchant's site, you will need a place to store these pages. This will also help you in building content, links, and a better search engine strategy with optimized content.

I have tried to keep costs as low as possible for you. I once read somewhere that Internet Marketing Guru John Reese said that you could start a business online for $250.

I can show you how to start one for 1/10 of that. You just need to apply a little elbow grease to get the same results. That's why you will find that many of the tools in this package are free. I think it is absolutely absurd to make people pay for software and tools that are readily available for free.

These resources have only been provided to show you EXACTLY how I market my business. I use the KISS principle. KEEP IT SIMPLE STUPID.

Introduction

Several years ago, when I started my business, I wish I had known what I'm about to teach you right now. I would have been a lot lot better prepared, and I would have started making money faster.

However, here is your chance to benefit from my experience, save yourself a ton of of time and money, and find out everything you need to know in one complete package.

Content vs. Non Content Strategies of Marketing

There are basically two ways to market your business online regardless of what type of business you choose to start.

You can use any combination of these strategies to both market your business, as well as create your websites.

The first thing you have to decide BEFORE you start an online business is: How much writing are you willing to do?

If you hate writing with a passion, and some do (I won't take offense because I'm a writer), then you only want to learn the skills you absolutely have to have to do the writing that needs to be done for your business. If you don't want to write at all, then you'll need to hire a copywriter.

If you don't mind a little writing, then you can exploit the Internet to do your marketing and do it absolutely free.

So, with a content strategy, you are using any combination of the following methods: blogging, article writing, newsletter publishing, free reports and ebooks, search engine optimization, linking, and press releases. All of these methods are largely free. You may have a content rich website that has plenty of articles, ebooks, reports, reviews, tips, and links to resources that you provide your site visitors.

A non content marketing strategy is straight advertising. This includes marketing methods like pay per click advertising, online and offline classified advertising, TV and radio commercials and others. With this method of advertising, you will be paying to advertise, and there is very little writing or content generation except to write your marketing materials (Information on how to do this is covered later under one of the steps).

Once you make a decision here, then you can go to the first step. With each step in this plan, you'll have all of the tools you need to complete that step. If you don't feel the need to use the tool, you don't have to download it. Just download what you need and use that tool to help you.

Small Business Software and Online Tools

For those of you who live in the United States, the Small Business Administration offers a **Small Business Planner**, <u>http://www.sba.gov/smallbusinessplanner/index.html,</u> you can use online. This is only necessary if you plan to apply for any type of financing for your business. You'll need to know all of the details included in this plan so that if you apply for financing of your business, you will be more likely to get it financed.

Even if you don't live in the United States, you can still use the business planning tools to help you create your business. This is, after all, about creating a plan for your business.

Now, if you don't need financing, your plan can be much simpler. Just write down what type of business you want to start: creating your own products, affiliate programs/MLM, services. Include what your topic of your business will be, and who will be your customer.

Once you've written down what your basic business plan will be, there are only two other tools that you will need for your business: accounting software and an affiliate program manager if you decide to market affiliate programs.

The easiest accounting software to use is **Banana Cash Book -** http://www.banana.ch/accounting/eng/download.shtml. It's freeware, works in multiple currencies, and is very customizable.

You can create your accounts so that you can keep track of income and expenses by account, and it's similar to keeping a checkbook register, so it's very easy to use. Basically, this program is single entry accounting. It's what I use to keep track of all my income and expenses, and I've had very good luck with it.

Keep in mind that when you download this software, it will ask you for a key. You don't need the key unless you plan to upgrade to the full software. Personally, I'm happy with the demo/Cashbook version as it makes it very simple for me to keep track of my business books.

If you market affiliate programs, it can be very hard to keep track of all your affiliate programs. By keeping track of all the affiliate programs that you're marketing, you'll be able to keep better track of your sales.

There's two ways you can do this.

1. Create a spreadsheet. You'll want to include the following categories: Program Name, Home Page Url, Affiliate Url, Category (i.e. Small Business, Web Hosting, etc if you market a lot of different affiliate programs), Program (if your program is part of a network like Click Bank or Commission Junction, you can use this to sort your programs to see how many you are marketing under a particular network), Commission Amount or Percentage, Payment Type (Pay Pal, check, etc.), How often you are paid (monthly, bimonthly, etc.), and a Comments section. In this section I usually put usernames, passwords, and any other relevant information I may need.

2. Use affiliate program management software. This software is getting harder and harder to find, but I recommend **Program Affiliate Manager**. It's freeware, and you can download a copy of it here: http://www.smallbusinesshowto.com/freeware/pam_full.zip

If you use this software, you can keep track of your income, as well as all of the details of the affiliate programs you are promoting.

Regardless of which way you decide to track your information, I recommend that you make paper copies of all this information so that if your computer crashes, you have good records, or you can backup your informaton. It's also a good idea to keep any receipts for any money that you spend so that you can prove your expenses, as well as keep track of all your expenses.

If you need to create any kind of custom forms for your business or website, then I highly recommend this site. It will allow you to create business forms in HTML for free: **http://www.createforms.com/**.

I keep all of my receipts and paper records in an envelope by year. I staple the paper record for the month, as well as all receipts and bank statements and relevant emails together. This makes it very easy to find things when I need them.

One other consideration you may have if you do decide to sell your own products is accepting checks and credit cards. By accepting credit cards, you can easily increase your sales by 50 percent or more.

Here are a couple of sites that I use. I've also included a site where you can make comparisons and find the solution that is right for you.

Clickbank –

http://www.jingerjarrett.com/recommends/clickbank. html - This site deals strictly with digital products, so if you offer tangible products, it won't work for you. However, it's a very inexpensive and easy solution for anyone who sells ebooks and software.

Pay Pal –

http://www.jingerjarrett.com/recommends/paypal.htm
l - I've had very good luck with this site, and in addition to
selling my products through Clickbank, I also use this site. You
have a lot more flexibility because you can offer monthly,
weekly, or any other type of periodic subscriptions, individual
products, and also tangible products. With 60+ million users,
and growing, you have a ready clientele available to buy what
you sell.

No Merchant Account -

http://www.nomerchantacct.com/ - You can use this site
to help you find merchant accounts and compare them.

One final note: you want to have a separate bank
account for your business, especially if you run a business in the
US. The IRS doesn't allow business and personal funds to be
mixed in the same account.

A bank account will be especially helpful if you use
services like Storm Pay or Pay Pal. This way you can download
your money directly into your bank account. Many affiliate
programs now offer direct deposit of your commissions, so this
is an easy way to do it.

If you're having trouble getting a bank account, then you
can do a search online for a second chance bank account. You
can still get a bank account even if you're on Chex Systems.
This is the easiest way I know of to get an account.

This last resource really doesn't really fit in unless you plan to sell affiliate programs, but it's just to good not to include.

Affiliate Money Machine will teach you everything you ever wanted to know about building an affiliate business, and it's free. You should know that unless you are already an expert in something, the fastest and easiest way to start your business is by marketing affiliate programs.

This free package contains the PDF ebook, Affiliate Money Machine, as well as a complete selection of videos you can watch to help you build your websites. You can download a copy here for free: **http://www.smallbusinesshowto.com/freeware/amm.zip**

The 7 Steps to Building Your Business In 7 Days

To make this book work for you, there are three things that I recommend you do.

First, print it out and read it all the way through. Make sure that you understand the material. My goal here is to make this as short, sweet, and simple as possible. You should be able to read this entire guide in a couple of hours.

When you are ready to apply the steps, do them one at a time. Complete each step and move on. Do it at your own pace.

If you already have a business, you may be able to skip some of the steps, but I would still recommend that you read through them to make sure that you have done everything that is covered under each step. This is to make sure that you have built a solid foundation for your business.

Keep a notebook. You will want to write down notes as you go along. I have included a checklist at the end of each section so that you can make sure that you have done each step. You can also write down notes here. Now, let's begin.

Day 1 - Select your product(s)

You have several choices here that you can make. You can choose affiliate programs, MLM, franchising, or you can create your own product or service.

There are two factors you should consider: what's popular and what your interests are. You will be with your business for a long time. Doing something you are passionate about will lead you to the money. Don't just choose a topic because it's high demand and low competition. When you get bored with it, you won't want to do it anymore.

However, you should also consider the fact that if there is no market for your product or service, there's no demand for it.

I know that there's been a lot of talk on the Internet about creating a niche. You can do this. What's not being said is that you should create a niche in something that is popular, as well as being something you are interested in.

That's why it's crucial that you do your research.

Below are several tools that you can use to help you in doing research for finding a product. You can also use these tools if you decide that you want to use pay per click search engines to promote your products and services, as well as optimizing your site for the search engines.

Lycos 50 Daily Report with Dean –
http://www.50.lycos.com - This daily column can help you spot trends on the Internet. Excellent resource if you are looking for new niches to exploit, and it can also help you with seasonal promotions for your products and services.

Yahoo Buzz – http://buzz.yahoo.com – This site is especially good if you plan to do any type of fan site and sell items related to a particular star, like books, Tshirts, and other affiliate products. Let me caution you though: if you plan to build a site around a particular person or group, you may not use that person's name or image in any way to create your own products. This is a violation of copyright. You can, however, find lots of affiliate programs that are legitimate that you can use to sell stuff related to that person or group.

Search Engine Tools -
http://www.submitexpress.com/tools.html – This site offers several tools you can use to not only legally spy on your competition, but you can also do keyword research. Keyword research is crucial to your success online. This will help you

drive targeted traffic to your website because your visitors are searching using the keywords you have optimized for.

SEOBook Keyword Suggestion Tool –

http://tools.seobook.com/keyword-tools/seobook/ - This site actually offers one of the best keyword research tools I've ever found, and it's very comprehensive. Even better, it's free, and the results you find will definitely help you find the right keywords for your websites and marketing campaigns.

Clickbank Search -

http://www.jingerjarrett.com/recommends/clickbank. html - You can browse the Clickbank directory to find out what products are hot.

The advantage of using Clickbank directly is that you can see when you are browsing which products are the most popular. This can help you in selecting affiliate programs, finding out what products have a market, and pricing any products you may create. This site only sells digital products, so keep that in mind. It won't help you with pricing tangible products, but it will pretty much tell you what there's a market for.

Read the descriptions on the different products carefully. You will find keywords here that you can use in your searches, and this will help you with any product research you do. You can also use other affiliate networks to help you with physical products. Here are two. You'll need to sign up for an account, but it's free.

Commission Junction - http://www.cj.com

Link Share -
http://www.jingerjarrett.com/recommends/linkshare.html

Toolbar Help

Which toolbar you use will depend on what you want to know. You may only need one or two, or you may need several as these toolbars will not only help you plan your business, but they will also help you when you get ready to market.

Try them out and see which ones work best for you. Then use that toolbar or toolbars to help you find your information.

Conduit – **http://www.conduit.com** – This site offers the most comprehensive collection of toolbars on the planet. You'll find thousands of toolbars on tons of topics. What I like about this site is that you can simply add new toolbars to your Conduit toolbar and switch back and forth. Many sites also offer toolbars they made at Conduit, including my internet marketing toolbar. You can get it here: Internet Marketing for Free - **http://internetmarketingforfree.ourbusinesstoolbar.com/**

Alexa - **http://www.alexa.com/site/download** - This toolbar is the best for helping you find information on your competition, as well as finding out which sites are linking to your competition. This toolbar also gives you the capability of searching Amazon. This can help you in finding different niche trends, as well as markets for your writing if you are a writer.

There are two ways to do a search here:

First, you can type in the domain that you are looking for. This will bring up a page with information on the site. You'll find contact information, traffic stats, ranking, and who is linking to that site.

The other way to get information is to do a keyword search. Sites will appear by rank. Each site will have a site info page so that you can see the traffic information. I like this site because it provides some of the most relevant information on your competition.

If you prefer not to use the toolbar, you can also go to the site and do your searches directly. This site is powered by Google, so it offers the most extensive search available in terms of how many sites, as well as how many pages, it has access to.

The next three toolbars are search engine specific. I have provided them for you based on your own search preferences. These three sites are the top search engines on the Internet. I would recommend that if you use any of these toolbars that you download your toolbar based on your own personal preferences and what type of information you are looking for.

Yahoo Toolbar – http://toolbar.yahoo.com

MSN Toolbar - http://toolbar.msn.com

Google Toolbar -
http://toolbar.google.com/index_xp.html

First, you use this toolbar to search Google.

If you market using Pay Per Click Search engines, especially Google Ads, you will find tons of resources included in this tool to help you with your search.

Public Domain Toolbar –
http://www.publicdomainforum.com/ - Whether you need content, or you want to find out what's available in the public domain, this toolbar will help you. It offers tons of resources, and will help you locate whatever you need within the public domain.

Software

Finally, the best tool I have found for doing both keyword research, as well as search engine optimization, is **Web CEO,**
http://www.smallbusinesshowto.com/search.html This is a complete suite of search engine optimization and submission tools you can get for free. It includes everything you

need to find keywords, optimize your website, and submit to the search engines.

This software works on both MAC and PC, and it comes with a free $97 search engine certification course, as well as complete documentation. If you can read and follow instructions, you can use this software to optimize your website for the search engines. There's also a quickstart guide you can read that will have you up and running in about an hour. It's in PDF.

Checklist

.1. Set up your accounting program or program to keep track of your affiliate programs.

.2. Select your affiliate programs or your products. If you are marketing affiliate programs, now is the time to add them to your software so you can easily keep track of them.

.3. Create your file system. This can be as simple as an alphabetical file system, or you can do it by date.

.4. Download and install any software you need to do your research. I use a very simple system on my computer, as well as my start menu to keep track of all of the various aspects of your business. Simply create five folders: Admin, Courses and Reading, Marketing, Website Updates, and Writing. You may call this last folder anything you like, but it will contain all of the documents and software related to your product creation.

Admin will contain all of the documents and software you use to keep track of your business. Accounting, files, etc. Courses and Reading are ebooks, videos, and anything else you have downloaded. Marketing contains your marketing plan, marketing documents and software. Website Updates contains everything you need for your website. Your Writing/Product Creation folder contains everything for keeping track of your products/services.

Day 2 - Select a domain name and web hosting

There are only two things you have to buy that I consider absolutely crucial to your success online: a domain name and web hosting.

What a domain and web site do for you is show that you are a professional, and it will also brand you, like Coca Cola, or some other name brand. If you are not willing to invest in your business, then why should anyone buy from you? That's how a lot of customers will think.

When choosing a domain, think carefully about what you are selling. If you will be marketing on Google Ads, and you have no desire to build a web site, just landing pages, then I would recommend buying your name or some variation. Then, all you have to do is upload your pages as you need them and send visitors to your landing pages. Since you can create unlimited subdomains on just about any web hosting account, you can create nice short links for your site. For example: http://blog.jingerjarrett.com. (This is just an example of what your link could look like, but as you can see, it looks better than an affiliate link.)

Whatever domain you choose, make sure it has to do with what you are selling. Pick something early in the alphabet. Whether you choose to hyphenate the words in it or not is your choice, but my experience has been that people often forget to include the hyphens, which could send them to someone else's site instead of yours.

Although many marketers will tell you to buy a domain that describes your business, most of the most popular domains online, like Yahoo and MSN, are names. Don't discount the value of a name.

When choosing your hosting, you need to consider what you actually need. If you are building a full blown website using a content management system, then you need hosting that supports scripts as well as MySQL databases. If you plan to host several domains, buy hosting that allows you to do this.

Below are my recommendations. Each of these solutions has been designed based on what direction you would like to take with your business.

Domains/Web hosting

Doteasy– http://www.doteasy.com - This site offers free hosting for the cost of the domain. There are also larger hosting packages with more tools, and it has a web site builder to build your web site so that you don't have to know HTML. The hosting is also very reliable, and you can use this site to start your business for only $25 a year.

Godaddy – http://www.godaddy.com - This is the most comprehensive of all the sites I offer. You have the option here of buying your domains separately and hosting them somewhere else. Godaddy also offers reasonably priced web site hosting in addition to promotion services and online storage. This is where I buy all of my domains. You'll find plenty of options here, as well as plans that fit your budget. This site also offers a web page builder.

Website.ws – http://www.jingerjarrett.com/recommends/websitews. html - This site specializes in both domain names and web hosting, but their real value comes from the affiliate program. You can use the affiliate program to build a full time, passive, residual income for your business in addition to whatever your primary business is. You also get a domain name, 10MB of web hosting, or you can forward your domain somewhere else.

The best thing I like about this site is that there are a lot of domains available here that aren't available under the .com extension. Also offers a web site builder with several videos to teach you how to set up your web site. (If you find the website builder to be a problem, I've added some tools for you to use to build a website).

Ultimate Marketing Center –

http://www.jingerjarrett.com/recommends/ultimatem arketingcenter.html - If you want to build an empire of multiple streams of income, then this is the site for you. You can host up to 21 domains per account, and you get 2GB of space. You get custom scripts you won't find anywhere else, as well as affiliate program management software, which no other web hosting offers. This feature alone will set you back about $45 a month.

It also offers unlimited autoresponders, unlimited email accounts, and search engine submission. There's also an extensive library of marketing software and ebooks, something that's not included in any of the other packages. Most of these packages you can sell, and you get new products each month. This collection alone is worth thousands of dollars and will teach you everything you need to know about marketing. What this site does that no other site I know of is offer you for this price is a complete business solution. You get all of the tools you need to build your business. The best part is that now you don't even need to know how to build a website. You can use Fantastico to install all of your websites.

Once you have selected your domain and web hosting, it's time to create your autoresponder. You need to do this before you create your web site because you will need the autoresponder code to integrate into your site. This is a simple step of cutting and pasting a little code into your web page.

Tip: When selecting a web hosting company that doesn't have a site builder, I would recommend that you select a web hosting company that offers Fantastico. Fantastico is a script installation system that will install most of the top content management systems and blogging systems for you, as well as lots of other scripts for your site. All you have to do is decide what directory you want your script installed in, and Fantastico will do the rest, including installing the script and creating the database. This will save you a lot of time, as well as eliminate the hassle of installing sites like Drupal and Wordpress.

Of the web hosts that I recommended, Ultimate Marketing Center is the only one that offers this. They also offer Soho Site Builder, which is the ultimate website building system. This system offers a complete content management system with a blog, newsletter generation, 100s of templates, and a ton of other great features. You can download it for free and install it as your content management system, or you can buy web hosting that offers installation of this script. You can find out more about this great free script here:
http://info.soholaunch.com/

Checklist

.1. Select your domain. You can use tools like the domain search tools at Godaddy to help you find domain names that are available and would be suitable for your business.

.2. Choose your webhosting. You will need to consider whether or not your are simply creating simple HTML web pages, or if you want to set up a content management system. If you use a content management system, you'll need to be able to run databases, and this is a feature that must be included. Do you want to host multiple domains or only one domain? The ultimate factor here is your budget and what you can afford.

Day 3 - Create an autoresponder

You have several options here. The services that I am recommending here I have both used. Both of the options are free. The autoresponders I currently use are supplied by **Ultimate Marketing Center,** http://www.jingerjarrett.com/recommends/ultimatemarketingcenter.html so this isn't another expense I incur.

I would recommend that you upgrade to a paid acount of some kind as soon as you can. Many free autoresponders make their money from putting ads in the header and footer messages. Get Response does, Free Auto Bot does not, but they do send you advertising.

Get Response - http://www.getresponse.com

Free Auto Bot - http://www.freeautobot.com/

You're probably wondering why you need an autoresponder.

Simple. You want to follow up with potential customers. By following up with your potential customers and building a relationship, you are more likely to make the sale. Also, if you aren't using an autoresponder, you're wasting traffic. Visitors will come to your site, and if they don't bookmark it, they may never come back again. This gives you a way to contact them again. By repeatedly exposing your list to your sales message, you will make the sale. It's this repetition and relationship building that will ultimately help you sell more of your products or services.

On average, you need to contact your potential customers about seven times with your offer. Statistically, over a period of one year, about 80 percent will buy.

Now, what should you include in your autoresponder?

You can offer a newsletter, ecourse, or a free ebook as a premium for subscribing. If you choose to create a newsletter, you can send out your newsletters on a regular basis when you write them, and you can also load the autoresponder with pre written sales messages, as well as free articles and free resources you recommend. Your pre written messages should be about a 50/50 split with content, which means that for every sales message you send out, you should send an article.

I would recommend that you write your own content, but if you don't want to, you can use article directories to help you find content to use. You can also use the public domain toolbar I mentioned earlier.

Here are three places to find content:

Go Articles - http://www.goarticles.com

Ezine Articles - http://www.ezinearticles.com

Article City – http://www.articlecity.com

There's also a handy free tool you can use called Orwell. This will tell you the keyword density of an article.
http://www.orwellpro.com/free-software.html

All of these directories contain a wide variety of articles on a wide variety of topics, so you can use the content on just about any subject you want.

If you do decide to use free articles, make sure that you include the resource box of the author and observe the copyright.

Once you have set up your web site, you'll want to copy the code for the subscription box to your autoresponder into a text document for use later. You'll find instructions on how to do this inside of the members' area of the autoresponder you choose.

Tip: If you decide to use articles by other writers in your autoresponder, I highly recommend you choose the best articles by writers who have affiliate programs. Most of these writers will allow you to change the link in the resource box to your affiliate link. This is to your advantage because it's an opportunity for you to earn an additional stream of income.

Checklist

.1. Do a search for autoresponder services. You can do this at any search engine. Study the various autoreponder services to find the one that suits your needs.

.2. Create the messages for your autoresponder. You should start with a series of at least seven different messages. These messages don't have to be long. Just make sure you include good content within the messages. Then include the link to the product you recommend.

.3. Space these messages about three days apart. You don't want to contact your potential customers too often, but at the same time, keep in contact with them on a regular basis. Always try to offer something of value.

.4. Upload these messages into your autoresponder. Each service contains documentation and help files to tell you how to do each one. All you will have to do is copy and paste your messages into the sequence.

.5. Copy and paste your autoresponder text for later use.

Day 4 - Build a website

The type of web site you choose to build will depend on several factors.

First is the product you are selling. If you are selling your own products, you can build a minisite. You can also build a minisite with an affiliate product, but you are better off building a theme based site around several different products than wasting a whole web site on one affiliate program.

Regardless of what type of web site you decide to build, all web sites have certain things in common.

Here is a list of things that you should include in your web site:

1. A contact page. Customers need to be able to contact you. You will get better results if you include a phone number, and even better, a real address because this gives customers confidence that if they need help, a real person is there to help. (Since I originally wrote this, I have learned that it's better if you use voice mail, especially if you don't have someone to answer your phone and you work at home. Some people just don't understand the time difference, and it's really no

fun getting phone calls at 3 am. You can get free voice mail from AIM.

http://free.aol.com/vox/)

2. A privacy policy. Customers want to know that you won't sell their information and that you will treat it confidentially. A privacy policy on site will instill this kind of confidence.

3. Clear information about what your site is about. For example, if your site is about fishing, don't include information about real estate, or some other topic. Stick to your topic. You can't be all things to all people, and having too many different topics on one site can be confusing.

4. A clear menu. Make it easy for your customers to navigate your site and find what they are looking for.

5. Don't make your visitor click more than three times to find what he/she is looking for. Otherwise, it makes it harder for the search engines to spider your site, and it will also make it harder for customers to find what they are looking for. If your customer can't find what he/she's looking for within two or three clicks, more than likely, he/she will click away.

6. Include a sitemap. This will help you get your site spidered by the search engines more quickly, and it will also help your customers find what they are looking for more quickly. You should also make sure that you include a link to your sitemap from the main page of your site. You can find plenty of free sitemap creators on the internet. Just type "free sitemap generator" into your favorite sitemap. Generate your sitemap according to the directions and then save it as sitemap.xml Once you have done this, upload it to your website in the root directory. Then you can submit it to Google and Yahoo. This will help you get your site indexed quickly, and you'll get a lot of traffic fast.

7. Include a subscription box to your newsletter or list. This should definitely be on the front page of your site, and if possible, on every other page of your site. This way you are more likely to get the potential customers to describe. Offer them a premium, or some type of freebie to subscribe. Make it valuable though so potential customers want to stay on your list.

8. Include a title, description, and metatags in the header of all your pages on your website. You would be amazed at how many sites forget to do

this, and then their sites are incorrectly indexed by the search engines, or they come up for the wrong search terms. You can use the tools at **Evrsoft,** http://www.evrsoft.com, to help you create the tags you need, and then all you have to do is copy and paste this information into the header of your web page.

There are two types of web sites you can create: content rich web sites and minisites. Instead of trying to teach you how to build each type of site, which would take about 100 pages, below are my best resources, all of them free, to teach you how to create the type of web site you would like to create.

Minisite Profits Exposed – http://www.minisitecreatorsecrets.com/main.html - This free video course by Michael Rasmussen will teach you how to build minisites that will actually make you money. This is a pretty comprehensive course with over 10 videos, but it's well worth the effort to watch these videos and learn how to build your sites.

Open Source CMS - http://www.opensourcecms.com/ - If you want to use a content management system on your website, then you'll find a wide variety here. The systems included here are all open source, which means that you can change them, as well as use them for free. This will help you decide if a content management system is for you.

Affiliate Masters Ecourse –

http://www.smallbusinesshowto.com/freeware/Aff-Masters.zip - Although Rosalind Gardner's ebook on marketing affiliate programs is very good, this free ecourse will teach you everything you need to know about building a content rich theme based web site built around affiliate programs. If you would like to see a content rich theme based site in action, check out Rosalind's **101 Date** - http://www.101date.com - on how to implement this strategy.

Service Sellers Ecourse –

http://www.jingerjarrett.com/ht/service-sellers.html - If you want to build a content rich theme based service site because you sell services, then this is the right ecourse for you. This is also a great ecourse for writers, business coaches, and others who want to bring their service businesses online.

Instant Internet Business –

http://www.instantinternetbusiness.com/ - If you are looking for a really good out of the box solution to starting a business, then try this. This site is content rich and search engine friendly, and you have a complete line of products at your disposal to sell. It's also highly customizable. (This site building system is also included as part of the Ultimate Marketing Center, and you can get it for free as part of your membership).

Affiliate Money Machine -

http://www.smallbusinesshowto.com/freeware/amm.zip - Although I've already mentioned this package before, I'll mention it again. If you need help building your website, these free videos will help, and you'll also get some great marketing tips and ideas too.

Search Engine Optimization Tools

There are four factors you need to consider in optimizing your site for the search engines that will help your rankings. They are: site optimization, linking, keywords, and content.

Below are my best tools, software, and resources for helping your optimize your site for the search engines, and implement these strategies. Mos of these tools are free.

IM Buzz Software – http://www.imbuzzcreators.com/ - If you want to download this free software, you will need to subscribe to the list. It's free. This is the most comprehensive pack of internet marketing software you'll find online. Really an incredible value. I use the Keyword Buzz software to help me find keywords. I would recommend you use all this softare in your business and you will make money.

Linking Matters – http://www.linkingmatters.com - If you want to implement a linking strategy into your search engine strategy, this free ebook will give you the strategies you need. This ebook offers step by step instructions on linking and why you need to use this strategy. Free. PDF.

Search Engine Optimization Fast Start – http://www.jingerjarrett.com/recommends/seofaststart.html - Now in it's fourth edition, and constantly updated, this free ebook will teach you how to quickly and easily become a search engine guru. It includes information on linking strategies, optimizing your site for the search engines, and it contains lots of free tools to help you with your search engine optimization. Free. PDF.

Web CEO Suite – http://www.smallbusinesshowto.com/search.html - Free Edition. This is one of the best pieces of software I've ever seen. It's hard to believe it's free. It has all of the tools you need to optimize your site for the search engines, a comprehensive help section with a step by step tutorial, and a search engine optimization course worth $97 included. Definitely worth a look if you plan to use search engines to promote your web site. Windows. Free.

Web Site Building Tools

These tools will help you build a web site, regardless of what type of web site you want to build, and they're all free.

Affiliate Defender -
http://www.smallbusinesshowto.com/freeware/affiliat
edefender.zip - Link cloaking tool for your affiliate program
URLS. This will help you increase your affiliate commissions by
providing clean URLs.

First Page 2000 – http://www.evrsoft.com - One of the
best free HTML editors on the Internet, this comprehensive
HTML editor offers four different levels of expertise from
beginner to expert. Hundreds of scripts included so that you can
add all kinds of interactivity to your site, comprehensive
instructions on how to use the software, and a preview so that
you can see what your document looks like.

Fly In Ads Creator –
http://www.smallbusinesshowto.com/freeware/flyinad
s.zip - You can use this tool to create a pop up subscription box
for your site. Just add your autoresponder code, create your
pop up, and past that code into your page. Very easy to use,
and it won't annoy your readers because it's very unobtrusive.
Similar to using Magic Subscriber.

HTML Kit – http://www.chami.com/html-kit/ - Whether
you are building your first web site, or you are a pro, you'll like
this HTML editor. It will actually point out errors in your coding
for you. Lots of features and lots of help with all kinds of
coding. It also works with the Firefox browser. Great

multipurpose tool you can replace your text editor with too. Lots of plug ins make this the most flexible text editor I've ever seen.

HTML Teacher –

http://www.smallbusinesshowto.com/freeware/teacher.zip - If you want to learn how to write HTML without a lot of fuss, then this tutorial will quickly and easily teach you how to write HTML. It's what I used to learn HTML, and it's one of the most valuable tools I have ever used.

Instant Site Creator –

http://www.jingerjarrett.com/recommends/myfreegiveaway.html - Whether you want to write a simple sales letter, or create a complete site, you can use this tool to do it without knowing any HTML. This is simply the best tool for creating a professionally designed site without hiring a copywriter or website designer. Just fill in the blanks and generate your site. Also includes tools for search engine optimization, joint ventures, and press release writing. (Since this is a free giveaway, you'll find a ton of other resources here to help you build your sites, get traffic, and make money. One of the best free giveaway sites on the internet.)

Niche List Builder – http://www.nichelistbuilder.com/ - Use this free tool to build lead capture pages to build your list. If you decide to use the system in Affiliate Money Machine, this is the best software for helping you build your list pages, and you can do it fast.

Pay Lock Pro –

http://www.smallbusinesshowto.com/freeware/payloc kpro.zip - This software will encrypt your Pay Pal buttons so that no one can steal your products. It will also help you automate the process of ordering your digital products. Works with Pay Pal subscriptions too. Windows.

Source Forge – http://www.sourceforge.net - This site offers thousands of open source scripts, content management systems, and software you can use absolutely free. It's one of the best resources on the Internet for finding tools for both your business and your web site.

Text to HTML – http://www.cyber-matrix.com/txt2html.html - Converts text documents into HTML. I use it all the time.

The Complete Web Authoring System for Windows, MAC, and Linux – http://nvu.com/index.php - This site offers a web site authoring tool similar to Front Page or Dreamweaver, but it's free. If you're looking for a way to create your web sites using Front Page or Dreamweaer, but you can't afford the price tag, then this software will give you the same functionality, and it comes in different platforms. (Please note: this package is currently being sold as VIP Site Builder. Don't buy that. Just download the free version and use it).

Web-It – http://x-volt.com/webit/downloads.html -
Simple drag and drop editor you can use to build your web site.
Lots of nice features and easy to use. Windows.

Tip: Before building your website, decide what type of website
you need. There's no need to download software, learn any
type of content management system, or anything like that if you
don't want to. If you're really serious about getting your
business started as soon as possible, you'll keep it as simple as
possible.

Checklist

.1. Your first step here is to decide what type of website you want to build. You can download all of the tools I have included in this package, as well as the tools I recommend, and try them out. Choose the one that works best for you and then begin building your site. Once you build your first site, it gets easier.

.2. Regardless of what type of site you decide to build, make sure you include a subscription box on your site and include it on every page. This will allow you to recycle your traffic. The truth is, most won't buy on the first visit to your website. By following up with your potential customers, you have a chance to build a relationship with them and make the sale because they will trust you.

.3. Optimize your site for the search engines and create a sitemap. Upload your sitemap to your website so your site gets spidered.

Day 5 - Write a marketing plan

There are two different ways you can promote your business online. You can use either one strategy or the other or combine both strategies for even more traffic to your site.

The first thing you need to decide is which, or both strategy you want to implement first. Then you will need to break it down into one technique at a time and implement one technique at a time. As you get one technique in place and seeing results, then implement another technique.

Now, you're probably wondering what I mean when I say strategy. At the beginning of this book I mentioned the content versus non content strategy. What you need to do is choose whether you will use a content strategy, which is usually free, or a non content strategy, which is paid.

There are exceptions though here, and I'll explain them later.

You can get a free tutorial on creating a marketing plan if you need it:

Marketing Plan Creation -

http://www.knowthis.com/tutorials/principles-of-marketing/how-to-write-a-marketing-plan.htm

You can follow the tutorial if you need a comprehensive marketing plan. This is usually only necessary if you need financing.

Below are the two strategies I just mentioned. I'll explain how you can get the most out of these strategies as a way to market your business online.

Content Strategy

With a content strategy, you are focusing on creating content for your web site, as well as to build value into your business. Unlike a non content strategy, you can use the content that you create to brand yourself as an expert and drive traffic to your site. By combining ebooks, articles, blogs, newsletters, and other written materials, you can also build a linking strategy where others are pointing back to you.

Article Magic –

http://www.smallbusinesshowto.com/freeware/article magic.zip - If you'd like to read some of the best articles ever written online by article writers and get some great marketing tips at the same time, then you definitely want to read this ebook. Edited by Priya Shah, it contains dozens of articles on internet marketing, as well as information on writing articles.

Marketing with Blogs Ecourse –

http://www.marketingwithblogscourse.com/ - It's rare to find many ecourses online that will really teach you anything. However, this offering from Priya Shah is different. You get real information on how to market on blogs, as well as a nice collection of the best free ebooks ever written on the subject of blogging. The nice thing is all the ebooks are PDF, making this ecourse accessible to everyone. If you only have time to take one ecourse, take this one.

Turn Words Into Traffic –

http://www.jingerjarrett.com/recommends/tunrwordsintotraffic.html - If you're serious about using articles to market your business online, and you want to generate thousands of new visitors to your site, as well as thousands of dollars in profits, then this is the resource for you. It's the most comprehensive resource online about writing articles. Although it's not free, it is well worth the money. PDF.

Writing For Publicity –

http://www.articlesubmissionsites.com - This is another ebook on writing articles that will help you further expand your skills. You have to subscribe to her newsletter, but it's well worth it.

Other forms of content include press releases, videos, audios, free reports you give away, as well as newsletters and ezines. You can archive these resources on your website giving your potential customers a reason to visit your site. You can also do a search in the search engines for these types of directories that archive this type of material. Not only will it help you build backlinks to your website, raising your rankings in the search engines, it also allows you to promote your content.

Non Content Strategy

With the non content strategy, you are using pay per click search engines, online/offline classified advertising, safelists, and ezine ads. This is traditional advertising. It can be very effective if you do it right. You can get a free ebook on writing classified ads when you log into your Traffic Swarm account.

Here are the tools I recommend you use to market online using a non content strategy. They're the most effective I've found, and they're all free.

5 Days to Google Profits –

http://www.jingerjarrett.com/recommends/5daysgoog leads.html - Free ecourse to teach you how to market using Google Ads. One of the best I've read.

Google also offers an ebook on writing Google Adwords. It contains worksheets, as well as instructions, to help you make the most of your Google Adwords campaigns. You can also use what you learn from this ebook to write ads for other pay per click search engines. You can download it for free: http://www.google.com/ads/library/maximimum_effect_dec03.pdf

7 Power Affiliate Tactics for Promoting Affiliate Programs –

http://www.smallbusinesshowto.com/freeware/amm.zip - This report will give you some great tips on how to market affiliate programs. I would recommend you download the report included, called *Striking Gold* because it has some of the best information I've ever read on marketing on Google Ads. HTML/PDF.

Free Ads Giveaway – http://www.freeadsgiveaway.com - How would you like 1000s of dollars in free traffic to your site? You'll find it all here.

Free Ad System –

http://www.smallbusinesshowto.com/freeware/freeadsystem.zip - You'll find plenty of places here where you can advertise your sites or business through free ezine advertising. Free ezines are an effective way to advertise because you can test your ads. Windows.

1000 Minutes of Free Internet Marketing Video – http://www.jingerjarrett.com/recommends/leadsleap.html – The most effective way to market your business online using the non content strategy is, of course, Craig's List. If you know exactly how to post and track your ads, this is the best system for helping you set up an almost completely automated marketing plan. It will take you about four hours using this system, but once you set it up, it takes about 15 minutes a day to maintain. Follow the instructions included in the ebook, as well as the video, and you'll be earning money in no time flat. (You'll need to sign up for an account, but it's free. Just log into your account, and click on the link in the left sidebar for "Bonuses". You'll find all of the videos here.)

Viral Marketing

Finally, I'd like to mention using viral marketing. Viral marketing is where you offer a freebie of some kind to promote your business. You make this freely available to your readers, and you allow them to give it away.

This can be a content or non content strategy depending on whether or not you write the content yourself. It really doesn't matter if you write your content or not, this strategy can still be just as effective if the readers perceive your freebie to be of real value.

The real trick here to starting a traffic virus is to allow others to brand your free offer before they give it away. This way, it gives them an incentive to promote your ebook, especially if you include affiliate programs to brand.

Checklist

.1. Using your notebook, make a list of marketing techniques you would like to try: search engine optimization, article writing, linking, forum posting, press release writing, safelists, ezine ads, etc.

.2. Choose one of these marketing techniques to try. Regardless of which one you choose, you need to submit your site to the search engines as soon as possible. You can use Web CEO to help you do this, as well as the list I have included on my website. Even if you use Web CEO, you need to submit your website to major search engines, Google, Yahoo, and MSN, manually. **http://www.jingerjarrett.com/Getting-Your-Site-Indexed-by-the-Major-Search-Engines/**

.3. Prepare to write your marketing materials. If you plan to use Google Adwords, or some other pay per click, you need to create a keyword list. Test and track each technique. If it doesn't work for you, or you don't feel the technique is doing what it should for you, try a new technique. This is how you build an effective marketing plan.

.4. If you want to really jumpstart your marketing plan in a big way, there are two things you can do: use Craig's List (see the videos), and download the free software from IM Buzz. Using this free software, as well as the free techniques outlined in Craig's List Marketer Pro, you'll get a ton of traffic for free.

Day 6 - Write your marketing materials

Once you have chosen the marketing technique, or techniques, that you want to use to market your business online, then you need to write your marketing materials. This will include things like solo emails, ads, articles, pay per click ads, press releases and any other materials you may need. You will save yourself a lot of time and effort if you write these materials ahead of time. Then you can simply copy and paste them when you're marketing, and it will go a lot faster. If you really want to speed up your marketing efforts and save a ton of time, you can get a free copy of Roboform Marketing from my members' area. This is what I use to market my business online, and it saves a lot of time: **http://www.killermarketingarsenal.com/ezine/**. Just sign up for a free account and click on bonuses.)

Before you do any writing though, it's a good idea to do some research. The easiest way to write great sales materials is to first decide what you want to write.

For example, if you decide you want to market using free classified ads, then you'll want to study free classified ads on the site you are marketing on.

Create a swipe file. This can be a simple text file with your favorite ads copied and pasted into it. You don't want to use others' ads to market your business; what you want to do is study those ads and then use what you learn from those ads and sales materials to write your own. Although this may seem time consuming, it's the most effective way to do it in the least amount of time.

Below are both online resources, as well as software, you can use to help you speed up the process of writing your marketing materials. I've also included what I think are the best ebooks available to you to help you learn how to write effective sales materials, as well as articles, press releases, forum posts, newsletters, and ebooks.

Copywriting Package –

http://www.smallbusinesshowto.com/freeware/copyw riting.zip - This package contains the essential ebooks you need to write copy for your business: *Autoresponder Magic*, *Million Dollar Emails*, and *Web Page Sales Letters Supreme*.

Article Creator – http://www.smallbusinesshowto.com/ freeware/articlecreator.zip - Use this program to actually help you write your articles. I take you through a step by step process where you fill in your title, bullet points, write a few paragraphs, and boom, you're finished. Works very well with Headline Search, which will help you find great titles you can copy. Windows.

Article Formatter –

http://www.fwointl.com/FWOFormatter.html - Use this online tool to properly format your articles before sending them to newsletter publishers. Great for writers because it will give you a word count, as well as formatting your article for email.

Forums Package –

http://www.smallbusinesshowto.com/freeware/forums .zip - You'll find a tool you can use to keep track of all your forums, ebook with 93 forums you can post on, and information on how to write forum posts. Windows.

Online Ezine Formatter – http://www.ossweb.com/ez-ezine-template.html - If you want a simple online tool you can use to create a newsletter, I've used this one, and it works great. Just type in your text, hit submit, and it outputs a nice text newsletter for you.

Online Email Formatter – http://www.formatit.com - Don't you just hate it when you get email, and it has all those little > > > > > > in it? This handy online utility will remove those marks and reformat the email to any width you like.

Online Sales Letter Builder –

http://www.pertinent.com/tools/letter-builder/sales/ - This online tool will help you to create a simple sales letter for your site or your marketing campaigns.

Free Press Release Builder – http://loska.com/release-builder.html – This free tool will help you write your press releases online. Using this tool will save you a lot of time, and you can write a press release in about five minutes.

Press Release Builder –

http://www.pertinent.com/tools/press-release/index.asp - Online press release builder that will help you write a press release.

Qumana Blog Publishing Tool —

http://www.quamana.com - This free blog publishing tool allows you to add image ads to your blog posts. You can use these ads in addition to Google Adsense on your blog because these are image ads. This editor is very easy to use and set up, and you don't need to know HTML. All you have to do is write your blog post and then publish. Free.

EMarketing Software –

http://www.emarketingsoftware.net/ - Run by internet marketer Randy Hastings, this site is one of the best collections of free marketing software I've ever seen. He has an excellent collection of tools to help you market on the pay per clicks, and you definitely want to get a copy of his free marketing ebook because he tells you how to market online. Lots of good information instead of a lot of the hype and fluff put out by the "gurus".

Free Ebay Ad Formatter –

http://www.auctionlotwatch.co.uk/auctionadcreator.html – Although this tool if for formatting ads for Ebay, you can also use it to format any kind of ads, especially if you are doing ads in HTML and don't know how to write HTML. This formatter will do all of the work for you, and all you have to do is copy and paste your ad into the appropriate form.

Free Ad Report –

http://www.jingerjarrett.com/recommends/freeadreport.html – You don't even have to write your own marketing plan. Bob the Teacher has created the most effective marketing plan available for those new to marketing, and he's giving it away free. If you don't know how to market, or you want to market effectively, start here.

ListDotCom.com –

http://www.jingerjarrett.com/recommends/listdotcom.html - List Building without a newsletter. This site will help you quickly and easily build a list. This site is very easy to promote, and I've had really good luck promoting with it.

List for Life –

http://www.jingerjarrett.com/recommends/listforlife.html – Not only can you use this site to help you quickly and easily build a list, but you get tons of free ebooks and software to teach you internet marketing, as well as promote your business on the internet, and you can even use the ebooks as free giveaways.

Traffic Swarm –

http://www.jingerjarrett.com/recommends/trafficswar

m.html - If you need a start page where you can quickly rack up credits to promote your site, I recommend this one. This site allows you to write text ads to promote your business. What I like the most about this site is that they often offer great freebies you can use to help you learn marketing or ad writing. Their promotions do change, so you want to log into your account frequently to download their latest offers. They're free.

Traffic Hoopla –

http://www.jingerjarrett.com/recommends/traffichoopla.html - This is the grandaddy of all start pages. It includes 30 start page exchanges and 20 safelists that you can market on. All of the traffic exchanges and safelists have been tested so that you get only the most effective ones online.

Checklist

.1. Before you start writing your marketing materials. Study where you are marketing. If you are using safelists, study safelist messages. Which ones intrigue you the most? Which products would you buy, and why?

.2. If you plan to write articles, press releases, or really any kind of advertising, make sure you include an intriguing headline. The headline is the most important part of your promotion, regardless of what technique you use. Keep a swipe file of headlines and rewrite them for your ads.

.3. When writing articles and press releases, make sure you include your resource box. This is absolutely crucial to driving traffic to your site. Make sure the resource you offer is related to what you are offering and provides more information and resources. Otherwise, you've wasted a valuable resource.

1. Study advertising. Whether it's sales letters, ads, email messages, or anything else, study them. Don't copy the actual messages, but use what you have learned to improve your writing, as well as improve your copy. Keep a swipe file of good advertising and use it when writing your own.

Day 7 - Implement your marketing plan

This is the final step in starting your business. If you have followed the steps, and I have given you plenty of tools along the way to help you, then you should have your new business in place. Although I set this up as a seven day plan, not everyone can implement it in seven days. Work these steps in order and master each step before you move onto the next one. By committing as little as one hour a day, you can have your new business up and running in no time flat.

Just remember it as seven steps. Seven steps to success.

Now, it's time to implement your marketing plan. Let me remind you that at this point, the most effective way to market is to first, implement one, and only one, internet marketing technique at a time. See how that works. Then move to the next technique and add it. Always test your results. If you find one technique that takes care of all your promotional needs, stick with it. Test it, refine it, and keep doing it. The most effective marketing is to always market consistently.

It's harder to do this on viral techniques like articles and ebooks, but you can look at your web logs to see how often something has been downloaded, and you can also type the title, or better yet, your name into the search engines, to find out who is using your articles or other resources. This can be a real eye opener as to what is really working for you.

Let me know what you think. Your opinion is very important to me. Use the convenient contact form on my site to tell me how to make this ebook better. I'll be happy to answer your questions, as well as help you:

http://www.jingerjarrett.com/support/

Below are more resources for you that you may need as you continue to do business online. All of them are free, and I believe that they will help you.

Miscellaneous Free Software, Ebooks, and Tools to Help You

Blaze FTP - http://www.flashpeak.com/blazeftp/ - If you need a fantastic FTP client to help you upload your website files, then you need Blaze FTP. This freeware client is the best one I've found to help you upload your files quickly and easily. Packed with lots of features, and it's very easy to use.

Doug Knox – http://www.dougknox.com - Have you ever had your start page on your browser changed to something you couldn't get rid of? Do you have other pesky problems that you just can't seem to fix? Then I highly recommend this site. Doug offers a wide variety of scripts that will help you protect your computer, as well as fix some pretty common problems. I've used them, and they work very well. Windows.

Driver Guide – http://www.driverguide.com - Need a driver for a piece of hardware or software for your computer but can't seem to locate one? Then try this site. You'll find tons of drivers for here for just about any software or hardware you can think of. It requires registration, but it's free to register, and you can download all of the drivers you need for free.

Freeware Home – http://www.freewarehome.com - This site offers over 7,000 different freeware programs that you can use on your computer. You'll find everything from business applications to hobbies, and they are all full versions of the software, not demos.

Gutenberg Project – http://www.gutenberg.org - Large repository of public domain material, mostly in text documents. Their goal is to make as many public domain materials as possible available on the Internet.

ICEOWS – http://www.iceows.com - My favorite zip utility. It will unzip just about any kind of zip file you can imagine, it supports multiple languages, and it's free. (Since most of the files offered in this ebook are in zip, you will definitely want to use this utility if you don't have one.)

Jans Freeware – http://www.jansfreeware.com - The is one of the top freeware sites online that's owned by an individual. It's easy to see why this site is so popular. You'll find all kinds of free ebook creators, as well as some nifty tools to help you with your web sites, and it's all free.

My Free Giveaway – http://www.jingerjarrett.com/recommends/myfreegiveaway.html – If you want the best software and ebooks to teach you how to write and promote articles, this site has the best collection. Not to be missed. You'll also find plenty of great tools to help you build your website, as well as your lists. If you choose one free membership site, make it this one.

Writing Cash –

http://www.jingerjarrett.com/recommends/writingcash.html – If you want to get started fast, then you need this site. This site will show you how to combine the power of Google Adwords, or any other pay per click search engine, and Clickbank. There's a 10 step tutorial to teach you exactly how to write your ads. Save your money on buying a Google Adwords ebook and use this tutorial. It's excellent, and best of all, it's free.

To get my latest free ebooks, promotion software, tools, and tutorials, make sure that you visit my blog, **Internet Marketing for Free:** http://www.askjinger.com. I update my blog almost daily, and you'll get all of the best free resources here.

Newsletters

American Writers and Artists Institute –

http://www.awaionline.com - This is one of my favorite copywriting newsletters. You'll find plenty of tips on writing copy, as well as writing assignments. There's also an archives and a forum on site, and their courses are top notch. If you want to be a millionaire, why not learn from one?

Copywriter's Roundtable – http://www.jackforde.com - This is another one of my favorite copywriting newsletters. It's always full of all kinds of information on copywriting, and Jack Forde pulls his information from some of the best copywriters in the business.

Publicity Hound – http://www.publicityhound.com – If you want to learn how to market your business using press releases, then Joan's comprehensive ecourse is absolutely the best. Over 80 lessons, she'll show you how to get the media's attention, as well as optimize your press releases for the search engines.

Writing for the Web – http://www.nickusborne.com - Written by Nick Usborne, this is a great newsletter for those who want to write copy for the internet and learn how to write search engine optimized copy. Nick just wrote a new ebook called *Writing for the Web,* and right now he's giving it away for free when you subscribe.

Updates

To receive updates on this product, you can go to:

http://www.jingerjarrett.com/lists/7dayebusiness.html

www.ingramcontent.com/pod-product-compliance
Lightning Source LLC
Chambersburg PA
CBHW071302170526
45165CB00003B/1389

* 9 7 8 1 4 4 0 4 1 5 0 8 1 *